Glory to God
in the Highest

Glory to God in the Highest

A Christmas Devotional

Oakridge Bible Chapel
2024

Glory to God in the Highest
A Christmas Devotional

Copyright © 2024 Josiah D. Boyd. All rights reserved. Except for brief quotations, no part of this book may be reproduced in any manner without prior written permission from the publisher. Write: Permissions, Proclamation Press, 2250 8th Line, Oakville, Ontario, Canada L6H 7E7.

Proclamation Press
2250 8th Line
Oakville, Ontario, Canada
L6H 7E7

www.proclamationpress.com

Unless otherwise noted, Scripture quotations are from the NASB® (New American Standard Bible®), copyright © 1960, 1971, 1977, 1995 by The Lockman Foundation. Used by permission. All rights reserved.

Print ISBN 978-1-0690570-0-6

General editor: Josiah D. Boyd
Cover Design: Colleen Wragg
Typesetting: Josiah D. Boyd

For all who celebrate and anticipate
the arrival of the Lord Jesus Christ.

AN INTRODUCTION TO THE DEVOTIONAL

Praise the LORD, all nations;
Laud Him, all peoples!
For His lovingkindness is great toward us,
And the truth of the LORD is everlasting.
Praise the LORD!

Psalm 117:1–2

I grew up in the Canadian prairies, "the land of the living skies," where the sunsets inflame the unobstructed horizon, the stars pepper the massive night canopy, and the northern lights dance in the dark. Although not typically considered as such, it *is* a place of natural beauty, uniquely curating God's creative handiwork.

To my shame, however, it took my moving away to fully appreciate the backdrop of my childhood. While there I remained unimpressed, unmoved, and largely uninspired. Was this because I was especially calloused, self-absorbed, and distracted? Maybe. But more likely it was because *familiarity breeds apathy.* The more we're exposed to something (even something fantastic!) the less special that something can become.

This is a perennial danger for the long-time follower of Jesus Christ, particularly when it comes to his history-shaping birth.

We hear it every year: "For a child will be born to us, a son will be given to us" (Isa. 9:6), "the Word became flesh, and dwelt among us" (John 1:14), and "when the fullness of the time came, God sent forth His Son, born of a woman" (Gal. 4:4). Mangers and Magi, angels and announcements, a star and a Saviour—same old, same old.

May it never be! How can we be unimpressed by the historical arrival of the long-awaited serpent-crushing Messiah? How can we be unmoved by God graciously wrapping himself in suffocating humanity to rescue sinful humanity? How can we be uninspired by the miraculous, mind-bending reality of the incarnation? Indeed, the first advent of Christ is a uniquely curated masterpiece of God's beautiful and loving handiwork.

The little book you hold in your hands is an attempt by God's people to fight the potential apathy brought on by our familiarity with the extraordinary. May our hearts sing the familiar song this season: "Joy to the world! The Lord is come! Let earth receive her King!"

It has been my privilege to serve and grow alongside the saints at Oakridge Bible Chapel for the last six years and to see and be the recipient of their love, thoughtfulness, grace, encouragement, and sincerity. It brings me joy to think that some of that will now be extended to you through what they have written in the following pages.

Glory to God in the highest!

Josiah Boyd

DECEMBER 1

HE MADE HIMSELF NOTHING

> Have this attitude in yourselves which
> was also in Christ Jesus, who, although He
> existed in the form of God, did not regard
> equality with God a thing to be grasped,
> but emptied Himself, taking the form
> of a bond-servant, and being made
> in the likeness of men.
>
> Philippians 2:5–7

The Apostle Paul is not commonly referenced in Advent liturgies, yet in his letter to believers in ancient Philippi, he invites us to ponder the doctrine central to our celebration of Christmas—the Incarnation.

Jesus, Paul reminds us, was in very nature God. He is the second person of the Trinity, the Word who was with God from the very beginning, through whom all things were created. All of heaven's resources were at his disposal; mighty angels bowed before him in adoration and hastened to do his bidding.

And yet, in one astounding act of selflessness, this King of glory *made himself nothing*. Other translations tell us that "he emptied himself." He who is infinite and complete in himself, who exists outside of time, and who spoke entire galaxies into being intentionally became finite. Constrained. *Limited.*

Christ chose dependence on a mother's breast and a stepfather's goodwill. He journeyed through the growing pains of childhood and adolescence. He had siblings and he cultivated friendships. Jesus knew hunger, thirst, exhaustion, labelling, disappointment, temptation, sorrow, and injustice. There is no aspect of human experience that Jesus has not tasted and to which he cannot relate.

And as he stepped into human history, Jesus adopted a particular posture: he took on himself the very nature, or essence, of a servant. Throughout the gospel accounts we witness Jesus serving. He uncorks a mysterious cache of wine to slake the thirst of wedding guests; he directs scores of fish into the empty nets of frustrated fishermen. With compassion he heals a friendless invalid; he calls back to life a dead man and restores him to his grieving sisters. And even as his own trial and crucifixion drew near, Jesus bent down to wash the mud-caked feet of the very ones who would desert him. Indeed, "the Son of Man did not come to be served, but to serve" (Matt. 20:28a).

As Christ-followers gathering to worship this Christmas, how can we rightly align our relationships with one another? We must begin with a steadfast gaze at the one who relinquished his rights, who made himself nothing, our humble Servant King.

Lord of Lords, help us to keep the unity of the Spirit through the bond of peace, leaning on your power, clinging to your wisdom, and looking to your Son.

Evelyn Pedersen

DECEMBER 2

A WONDROUS SCENE

> "This will be a sign for you: you will find
> a baby wrapped in cloths and lying
> in a manger."
> Luke 2:12

Each year, as I prepare to set up my Nativity Scene in the front foyer of our home, I am reminded that the Christmas story never grows old. It will always remain a treasure in my heart and something I will treasure each year.

As I carefully set each figurine in place, I see the baby Jesus lying in the manger with his earthly parents, Mary and Joseph, kneeling lovingly by his side. I now place some of the farm animals in the background so that our attention is fully drawn to the newborn babe.

On the rooftop, I have propped a shining star over the stable that twinkles brilliantly. The shepherds will soon arrive as they have recently gazed up at an unusual but magnificent phenomenon in the night sky. They wonder to each other, "Why such a spectacle? What does this mean? Shall we go?"

In the forefront of the stable area, I have placed one of the camels that brought the Wisemen from the East bearing gifts of gold, frankincense, and myrrh. King Herod had given orders for them to find the child who was born to be King of the Jews and now they are here on bended knee.

On their journey, they were led by the star that now rests over the place where Jesus lay. Scripture tells us that God revealed to these Wisemen in a dream not to travel back the same way they had come as Herod had murderous intentions (Matt. 2:1–12).

Outside the manger scene, I have placed a shepherd boy carrying one of his lambs with others following closely behind. Now, two of the little animals wander up close and lay down beside the Lord's makeshift crib. I ask myself, "Did this young shepherd know to whom he was approaching? As he peered inside the stable, did he wonder if this could be the promised and anticipated King? Is he the one who will die for my sins?"

How appropriate this all seems! Shepherds welcoming the Great Shepherd. Wisemen worshipping he who is Wisdom! Many worshipful thoughts fill my mind as I put each figurine in place. I am thankful for all that Jesus Christ has done in my life. Thank you, Lord, for coming to earth to be the Saviour of the world.

Lord Jesus, may the wonder of your incarnation never fade, the beauty of your condescension never pale, the sweetness of your humiliation never wither, and the power of your love never dull.

Nancy Jones

DECEMBER 3

WHAT ABOUT JOSEPH?

> Train up a child in the way he should go,
> Even when he is old
> he will not depart from it.
>
> Proverbs 22:6

When we consider the birth scene of our Lord, we pay due respect to the lowly shepherds huddled around the manger as they cast wonderous eyes on the newborn infant, as they marvelled at what had been told them about the King of Israel. We wonder what was going through the mind of Mary as she sat amazed at what had transpired over the last nine months.

But what about Joseph?

Many can name a Christmas carol devoted to Mary, the mother of our Lord. But can you name even one devoted to Joseph?

We read of one angelic visit to Mary and her submission to the news. But what about Joseph? We read of many angelic visits to Joseph and how he obeyed every commandment given to him. Joseph took charge of his family and their needs, so he deserves our admiration.

Proverbs 22:6 reads, "Train up a child in the way he should go, even when he is old he will not depart from it." Because Joseph was a godly man, he was an excellent choice to be an example of manhood for the child Jesus as he grew up.

Matthew also makes clear that Joseph was a loving and merciful man, refusing to bring public disgrace on Mary. Rather, he planned to hide what he thought was sin on her part: "And Joseph her husband, being a righteous man and not wanting to disgrace her, planned to send her away secretly" (Matt. 1:19). Joseph acted according to Scripture where we read that, "Lovingkindness and truth have met together; righteousness and peace have kissed each other" (Ps. 85:10). Joseph planned to act with undeserved grace by putting Mary away privately not disgracing her in public. Also, he was acting in truth by putting her away as the Law prescribed.

Jesus acted like his legal father, Joseph, because he always did what his Father in heaven prescribed (John 8:29). So why is Joseph largely ignored during the Christmas season and, for that matter, throughout the entire year? Why is he not extolled as a wonderful example of a godly father?

What about Joseph?

Heavenly Father, thank you for the gift of earthly fathers and father-figures who model your love, grace, and truth. Help us take up that same mantle, encouraging and loving those around us.

Gordon Rumford

DECEMBER 4

TO: JESUS—LOVE: US

> For God so loved the world, that He gave
> His only begotten Son, that whoever
> believes in Him shall not perish,
> but have eternal life.
>
> John 3:16

One of our family's favourite Christmas traditions began after I read the children's book, *The Sparkle Box*. The idea of the book is to get the most sparkly gift box you can find, fill it with slips of paper that are personal gifts for Jesus, wrap it in a bow and place it under your tree. When we started this tradition, our boys were quite young, so it was a wonderful way to teach them that Christmas was about celebrating Jesus' birthday. Before they started making their own Christmas lists, we wanted to take time to think about the special gifts we each could give our Lord and Saviour.

John 3:16 tells us of the greatest gift God bestowed on humanity. God's love for us was so great that he gave his one and only Son, Jesus, to be the sacrifice for our sins. Since God is holy, our sins were separating us from him and those sins needed to be atoned for.

In the Old Testament, sacrifices included animals that were without blemish or stain. Jesus was without any sin which made him the perfect substitute for us and the ultimate atoning sacrifice. Jesus willingly took our sins upon himself and washed them away by his blood. In doing so, he appeased God's judgment and reconciled our once broken relationship. Our belief in Jesus' death on the cross and resurrection gives us an eternal and glorious hope. The acceptance of this free gift gives us assurance that we are forgiven and that one day we will be in heaven enjoying everlasting life with our Saviour.

Are you wondering about the gifts in our sparkle box? They have changed quite a bit over the years. When our boys were little the gifts included sweet hand-drawn pictures and Jesus' name in early printing. Later, the gifts included items purchased for families in need, decisions to put away devices, and promises to devote more time to praying and reading God's word. Every year we try to give Jesus gifts that we think he would love. After all, he is the best gift we have and will ever receive.

Lord, we will be forever grateful for the most precious gift we've ever received, the gift that you so graciously gave to us, the gift of yourself. We love you, desire to be like you, and long to see you.

Marie Mathew

DECEMBER 5

COVENANT FAITHFULNESS

> "I see him, but not now; I behold him, but not near; a star shall come forth from Jacob, a scepter shall rise from Israel, and shall crush through the forehead of Moab, and tear down all the sons of Sheth."
>
> Numbers 24:17

Israel, having been rescued by Yahweh and set free from their taskmasters in Egypt, were on their way to Horeb. There they would meet with the God that had saved them with great signs and wonders, the God who is their vanguard and rearguard, a pillar of cloud by day and fire by night. He's the God who delivered the beleaguered nation and split the sea so they may walk on dry ground, who displays his great power and yet condescends to meet them and covenant with them and promises to bless them with a land of their own.

Despite their grumbling and testing of Yahweh, he lovingly disciplines them and rescues them in several notable battles. Balak, King of Moab, wishes to secretly invoke a curse upon this seemingly unstoppable army and calls upon Balaam the prophet for spiritual aid.

But Balaam, who at great lengths and threats by Yahweh, agrees to say whatever Yahweh would permit and not what Balak requested. The prophet tries to curse Israel three times but ends up blessing the nation instead. After extolling Israel's righteousness (which didn't exist, since they constantly complained against Yahweh) and promising an enduring legacy (which wasn't apparent since they were not yet in the promised land) we see the crux of the blessing—the King of Israel (the first of whom wouldn't be installed for centuries). Yahweh's faithfulness to Israel is secondary to his faithfulness to the Seed promised from Eve to Abraham and his sons. An outpouring of that faithfulness is the Messianic King and his salvific work to Israel and the nations.

At a time when Israel was faithless in dealing with Yahweh, Yahweh remained faithful to Israel. He proclaimed that the sign of the promised seed would be a star and that, while most of Israel would remain faithless, Yahweh would display his faithfulness and lovingkindness by sending the second person of the Godhead, the Son, as King of Israel to bring peace and righteousness to the nation and then to all the world.

This Christmas let's remember that we are undeserving beneficiaries of the love shared by the members of the Godhead and that it is their faithfulness that we are now called to imitate.

Father, may Christ dwell in our hearts through faith this season, that we may be able to, along with all the saints, more fully comprehend the unmerited and divine love of our Saviour.

Melvin George

DECEMBER 6

SAVOUR THE SAVIOUR

> O taste and see that the LORD is good;
> How blessed is the man
> who takes refuge in Him!
> Psalm 22:2

The sights, savours, and smells that are embedded in our memories during the Christmas season are nothing short of precious.

Unless you are in a season of loss.

I recall very vividly my first Christmas as a young woman of 38—with two teenagers and a gutted heart after my 20-year marriage came to a brutal end. All my dreams of seeing my grandchildren play with my children's toys in their childhood home came crashing down. My heart was shattered. Previous Christmases were filled with traditions from two different cultural backgrounds. Our gatherings were filled with marvellously tasting food mingled with overlapping conversations and chaos! Oh, how my heart ached for my kids! My dear extended family did their best to carry on as if nothing had happened, but their sadness was also palpable.

Nothing felt, smelt, or tasted good that year. I could see people chatting and hear their laughter. I could see the tables filled with delicious food—the aroma permeating throughout the house—but I felt numb, angry, and anxious about the future. I can recall asking the Lord "What's wrong with everyone? Can't they see I'm bleeding? Don't they see our loss? Why are they so happy?!"

Through it all, Jesus was my constant. I believed with all my heart what Romans 8:28 said, that everything would work together for *my* good. I immersed myself in reading the Bible and singing praises with tears flowing freely. Nothing else brought me comfort. I was trusting him.

My Saviour, who was born to die, was holding me, guiding me, and comforting me.

I learned to savour the Saviour; to consume his word and take his promises to heart. The moments I spent talking to Jesus and clinging to his many promises were precious to me. The more I focused on him, the smaller my circumstance became. I gained a deeper insight into the character of God. By reading his word, I found wisdom, courage, and strength for my daily dependence on him.

Friend, if you find yourself in a season of loss during this Christmas, let me encourage you to savour the Saviour. Taste and see that the Lord is good. You will still have moments of sadness, hurt, and loss on this side of eternity, but you will also experience his perfect peace and joy—a taste of what is yet to come in our heavenly future!

Father in heaven, you are as good to us are you are present with us. Thank you for being a God who draws near to the broken-hearted, a God who grants peace, comfort, and healing.

Gisella Giraldi

DECEMBER 7

A VISIT FILLED WITH BLESSING

And [Elizabeth] cried out with a loud
voice and said, "Blessed are you
among women, and blessed
is the fruit of your womb!"

Luke 1:42

We are being given a window into an intimate encounter between two women who were experiencing great change. Elizabeth was about to be a senior new mother and Mary was about to be a virgin new mother. It's likely that both women felt uneasy, thinking about the coming changes.

Yet what did they focus on? Not their own fears. They *blessed God* and they *blessed each other*.

Elizabeth blessed Mary by confirming God's truth in her life (1:44–45), and she blessed Mary's unborn son, Jesus, by acknowledging him as her Lord (1:43).

Mary glorified the Lord in praise (1:46–49), and blessed Elizabeth by sharing the presence of Jesus within her (1:44). Both women were able to do this because the Holy Spirit spoke and acted through them.

When we spend time with Christian sisters and brothers, let's have intention. Beyond enjoying ourselves, do we consciously look for opportunities to *bless God* and to let the Holy Spirit *bless each of us* through the other?

As we prepare to be with people this season, let us pray ahead and ask God what he would like us to say or do that will *bless him* and *bless them*. While with others, we can actively ask ourselves, "How can God be blessed through what they are saying?" and "How is God blessing me through them?" Or if someone contacts us with a practical matter, maybe our response can also include *blessing God* and *blessing them*.

Christmas is an ideal time to *bless God* for his wonderful gift of Jesus our Lord, and to *bless others* by sharing how amazing that gift is.

God in heaven, while we live in a culture characterized by consumerism and individualism, help us to be mindful of others, looking for opportunities to love them as you have loved us.

Carol Nowak

DECEMBER 8

MAJESTY IN THE ORDINARY

> But as for you, Bethlehem Ephrathah,
> too little to be among the clans of Judah,
> from you One will go forth for Me to be
> ruler in Israel. His goings forth are from
> long ago, from the days of eternity."
>
> Micah 5:2

Micah's prophecy speaks of an unlikely place—Bethlehem, a small and insignificant town—where the greatest of kings would be born. As one king sits on a throne as the ruler and emperor of the greatest power on the face of the earth in Rome, a second king comes not in power and majesty, but in humility. The Saviour who could have come in grandeur and splendor, instead, chose to enter the world in simplicity, born in a manger—a backdrop of humiliation.

As we reflect on this, we are invited to consider how God works through the ordinary. In our own lives, we may feel insignificant, unnoticed, or unimportant, yet God sees us. Just as he chose Bethlehem, he chooses us to be part of his redemptive story. The birth of Jesus in Bethlehem points to the reality that God's power is made perfect in weakness, and his grace is for all.

This coming ruler will "shepherd his flock in the strength of the LORD" (Mic. 5:4). Jesus, our Good Shepherd, leads us with gentle strength. He is not distant or uncaring; he walks with us, guides us, and protects us. In a season where we may feel the weight of the world's chaos or personal struggles, Advent is a time to return to the Shepherd who offers rest and security. We are reminded that our peace does not come from circumstances, but from the presence of Christ.

"[Jesus] will be our peace" (5:5). Jesus doesn't just bring peace; he *is* peace. He reconciles us to God and, through him, we find wholeness and rest. This Advent, as we prepare for Christmas, let us invite Christ's peace into every corner of our lives. Whether we are facing anxiety, uncertainty, or busyness, we can rest in the assurance that the Prince of Peace is with us, and that his reign will have no end.

May this Advent season fill us with awe and hope as we reflect on the humble King who came to save us and guide us into eternal peace.

Our Father in heaven, may the overwhelming peace of Christ—he who is peace personified—rule in our hearts this season since, as members of one body, we have been called to just that.

Avery Pham

DECEMBER 9

THE PEACE OF IMMANUEL

> "Behold, the virgin shall be with child and shall bear a Son, and they shall call His name Immanuel," which translated means, 'God with us.'"
>
> Matthew 1:23

The scene described in Matthew 1:18–25 is incredibly fascinating. Come rediscover it with me.

Mary and Joseph are engaged to be married and, as was customary at that time, Mary would go home, pack her things, and wait for Joseph to come to get her for the wedding. The bride-to-be may wait two weeks or even six months. Joseph, during this time, was preparing the home that they would soon share, as well as the wedding tent.

Imagine, if you will, being a few weeks into these preparations when you find out that your *bersherta*, your *betrothed*, your *fiancée*, is pregnant and not by you. I have no idea what Joseph must have been thinking but I'm sure his mind must have been all over the place, wondering if he should go through with the marriage at all. What would his parents say? What would the community say?

At just the right time, an angel of the L-rd* shows up in a dream and lays it all out for Joseph amid this chaotic storm. The baby growing inside of Mary is from the Holy Spirit. He is no ordinary baby! This baby is to be named "Immanuel," meaning "G-d with us."

In Jewish naming traditions, the name given to a child usually has family significance that highlights character traits seen in the child or hoped for in the child. In other New Testament passages this child is named "the Son of G-d," "Yeshua" (or "Jesus" referring to the salvation he would bring to the world), or, as in this passage, "Immanuel."

During the wedding chaos, "G-d with us" brings his *shalom*, his peace. His presence calms the storm. The angel knew Joseph needed that peace and to have his thoughts and fears stilled. That's exactly what the L-rd provided through the angel.

This Christmas may your thoughts and fears be calmed by his *shalom*. May you accept Immanuel: G-d with us!

Immanuel, you are our peace in the chaos of life, our mooring in the storms of this world, and our surety in the uncertainty of our days. Help us draw near to you even as you draw near to us today.

Susan Hawkins

---

* Editor's note: some believers avoid writing full divine names to guard against taking them in vain (e.g., Ex. 20:7) and as an expression of their reverence for him of whom they speak.

DECEMBER 10

THE ADMIRABLE CHARACTER OF JOSEPH

> And Joseph her husband, being a righteous man and not wanting to disgrace her, planned to send her away secretly.
>
> Matthew 1:19

As we celebrate the birth of Jesus, we can learn and benefit from considering some of the many character traits of his earthly father, Joseph, a man who showed himself to be a righteous and obedient leader.

Mary, the mother of Jesus, was pledged to be married to Joseph (Luke 1:27) but, before they came together, she was found to be pregnant by the Holy Spirit (Matt. 1:18). Joseph didn't want to expose her to public disgrace and, instead, had a mind to divorce her quietly (Matt. 1:19). "But when he had considered this, behold, an angel of the Lord appeared to him in a dream, saying, 'Joseph, son of David, do not be afraid to take Mary as your wife; for the Child who has been conceived in her is of the Holy Spirit'" (Matt. 1:20). When Joseph awoke, he did what the angel had commanded and took Mary as his wife (Matt. 1:24).

This beautiful scene shows that, with God's assurance, there was no hesitation by this man. Joseph was righteous—good, just, and upright before God—and willing to be obedient to God. Today, we hear God speak in the pages of the Bible and must, like Joseph, be willing to act in accordance to what his Spirit reveals and to pursue the righteousness demonstrated by Joseph.

After resolving to obey, Joseph made the necessary plans to take Mary to Bethlehem to register for a census (Luke 2:1–5). When they arrived in Bethlehem and found "no room for them in the inn" (Luke 2:7), Joseph set about finding the best alternative available. Later, he heeded God's warning to take Mary and Jesus to Egypt, running from the murderous Herod (Matt. 2:13–15). There was no delay in Joseph's obedience to the divine command. In fact, waiting would have likely meant the death of the child. A trip to Egypt had its dangers, but that night he "got up and took the Child and His mother while it was still night, and left for Egypt" (2:14). Jesus's earthly father acted with obedience and without hesitation.

When we respond to God's leading in our lives, we also must sometimes take a risk in our obedient actions, confident that God is leading us for our own good and for the benefit of others. And, seeing as that child would end up bringing salvation to the world, we certainly benefited from Joseph's righteous and obedient leadership!

Lord, we are grateful for examples of godliness—men and women who live lives characterized by obedience, submissiveness, courage, and kindness. Help us, we ask, follow their lead and, in so doing, become more like your Son, Jesus Christ.

Melissa Yang

DECEMBER 11

THE HEART OF CHRISTMAS: SHARING GOD'S LOVE

> After coming into the house they saw the
> Child with Mary His mother; and they fell
> to the ground and worshiped Him.
> Then, opening their treasures, they
> presented to Him gifts of gold,
> frankincense, and myrrh.
>
> Matthew 2:11

Growing up in India, Christmas was synonymous with the spirit of sharing, especially for my parents. My mother would meticulously prepare an array of treats and snacks in advance, ready to be distributed to our neighbours on Christmas Day. I vividly recall returning from the Christmas church service to find people waiting outside our home, eagerly anticipating the treats. Although my parents were not affluent, they generously shared their food with those less fortunate, seizing the opportunity to convey the true meaning of the season. Remarkably, they have preserved this tradition to this day, embodying the essence of giving each Christmas.

Christmas is a time deeply associated with the traditions of giving and sharing. In Matthew 2:11, we read about the Magi, men of means who journeyed from distant lands to behold the newborn King. Upon their arrival, they did something extraordinary—they opened their treasures and presented the baby Jesus with gifts of gold, frankincense, and myrrh. These offerings were not mere tokens of respect but symbolized the reverence and love the Magi had for the child. Their act of giving teaches a profound lesson about the heart of Christmas. Genuine sharing transcends the mere exchange of material gifts. Instead, it is about offering what we cherish most with love and reverence. Just as the Magi shared their treasures with Jesus, we too are called to share our blessings with others, reflecting God's love in all that we do.

This season let us ponder how we can extend our generosity beyond just presents. Can we dedicate time to someone who is lonely? Can we lend a hand to those in need? Can we offer words of encouragement and love to those around us? By giving in these simple ways, we mirror the generosity of the Magi and, more importantly, the boundless love of God, who gave us the greatest gift of all—his Son.

As we share this Christmas, let us do so with hearts overflowing with love and gratitude, recognizing that in giving we are not only participating in the true spirit of the season but sharing God's love with those around us.

Our Father above, from whom comes every good and perfect gift, thank you for your generosity to us. Help your people, filled with your Spirit, to increasingly mimic this grace to those you place around us.

Mani Kunadian

DECEMBER 12

AN AMAZING CHILD OF PROMISE

> For to us a child is born, to us a son is given, and the government will be on his shoulders. And he will be called Wonderful Counselor, Mighty God, Everlasting Father, Prince of Peace.
>
> Isaiah 9:6 NIV

Isaiah 9:6 is one of the most well-known and often-cited prophecies, particularly at Christmas time. Long before the shepherds received the good news of great joy, Isaiah predicted that a child would be born to us.

This sounds hopeful and majestic but, at the same time, perplexing. A child? And yet this child was predicted to be remarkable, called "Wonderful Counselor, Mighty God, Everlasting Father, Prince of Peace" and so many other powerful names. Let us ponder together this amazing child.

"For to us a child is born, to us a son is given, and the government will be on his shoulders." God promised to come to us as a child. The "us" refers to the people of Isaiah's time but to the people of our time as well. This child will be a ruler who will bring deliverance, light, and joy to the people of God.

He will be a "Wonderful Counselor," a counselor who is wise. He has wonderful wisdom that is beyond our imagination. The child will be a counselor who knows how to apply wisdom in every situation on our behalf. His wisdom is impressive. He knows what is best for us.

He will be called "Mighty God." God's love has the power to speak creation into being, to raise the dead to life, to part the seas, to make the blind see, and to heal diseases. The promised child's throne of peace and dominion will be established forever. His mighty power is derived from the fact that he is God himself.

Then there's "Everlasting Father." God will be with us forever. We do not trust in a God who is momentary. We are putting our trust in a God who is eternally paternal and that gives us hope.

As "Prince of Peace" Jesus will provide peace to us spiritually and in our human experience. He alone gives perfect peace, something things and people cannot do.

This amazing child has already been given to us. While we wait for our blessed Saviour's return, we must intentionally share the reason for our hope with those who do not know him. As we approach the Christmas season, let us focus on the blessings of the birth of the Christ-child. May our hearts bow in humility and gratitude to the Wonderful Counselor, Mighty God, Everlasting Father, and Prince of Peace.

Our great God, our world desperately needs wise counsel and enduring strength, eternal security and lasting peace. Our hearts are filled with thanksgiving and joy knowing that it's all available in your Son.

Shantee Singh

DECEMBER 13

JOY INEXPRESSIBLE

> … and though you do not see Him now,
> but believe in Him, you greatly rejoice
> with joy inexpressible and full of glory.
>
> 1 Peter 1:8

Have you ever been searching for something and not known exactly what you were looking for? Maybe it was a career, a home, or a spouse. Perhaps you had a vague idea of what you needed or wanted and you hoped you would be able to recognize it when you saw it. There might have been a slight trepidation or even fear that it might pass you by if you were not looking closely enough. Oh, the very thought that it stared you in the face and you missed it! It might have even happened that you thought you found what you were looking for, but hesitated, because of a nagging doubt in the back of your mind. I would like to venture a guess that we all can relate to one or more of these feelings and scenarios. It could be that this holiday season you find yourself right in the middle of it.

At various points of Advent, I have often marvelled at the story of Simeon. Scripture says that he was "righteous and devout, looking for the consolation of Israel; and the Holy Spirit was upon him" (Luke 2:25). Reading further it says that he had been promised that he would not meet death until he had "seen the Lord's Christ" (2:26), or the Messiah. I often have wondered if he knew exactly what he was waiting to see. Was it the newborn that he finally saw? Did he know that Messiah would be a baby? Unfortunately for my curious mind, the Holy Spirit leaves us in the dark of Simeon's inner workings but what we can read and know for certain is that, by the power of the Holy Spirit, he most certainly recognized the fulfillment of God's promise when he laid his eyes on the child. He did not die wondering if he had missed it. The passage says that he "blessed God" and even spoke to the future of what God intended to fulfill through his Son, Jesus (2:28–32). Seeing God's promise fulfilled made Simeon see even farther, to more of what God had promised.

As believers, we find ourselves in a very similar position as Simeon. We are all hoping and waiting for our final deliverance and the second coming of our Lord. We have the promise that, "The one who raised the Lord Jesus from the dead will also raise us with Jesus and present us with you to himself" (2 Cor. 4:14 NIV). It is something wonderful that we are eagerly anticipating. Through the comfort of God's Spirit and God's word, in the words of 1 Peter 1:8, we can love him, believe in him, and rejoice with joy inexpressible.

But still we wait. And I hope that this Christmas season, as you meditate on the wonder of God who became flesh, the hope of eternity in his presence and the redemption of your soul will leave you looking and longing for more of God. I hope that this Christmas season, regardless of the circumstance in which you find yourself, you will be peace-filled, knowing that his promises to you are as sure and concrete as Simeon's were. You will not miss them.

Come, Lord Jesus. This is the cry of your people. As we look back in thankfulness we look forward in anticipation. We long to see you truly and know you fully.

Becky Vellekoop

DECEMBER 14

RUTH AND A DNA OF LOVINGKINDNESS

> Who, although He existed in the form of God, did not regard equality with God a thing to be grasped, but emptied Himself, taking the form of a bond-servant, *and* being made in the likeness of men.
>
> Philippians 2:6–7

Ruth is a story of refugees returning to Israel. One, Ruth, makes a vow to Naomi and her God, Yahweh: "But Ruth replied, 'Don't ask me to leave you and turn back. Wherever you go, I will go; wherever you live, I will live. Your people will be my people, and your God will be my God. Wherever you die, I will die, and there I will be buried. May the LORD punish me severely if I allow anything but death to separate us'" (Ruth 1:16–17)!

Ruth's vow to Naomi, a reflection of the divine nature of *lovingkindness,* records a human DNA. Her freely given commitment sustained Naomi's life and prompted a landowner, Boaz, to extend safety in the harvest field and meals with his harvesters (2:8–9). Boaz, recognizing Naomi's need, accepted the role of kinsman-redeemer (4:6), *re-purchased* Naomi's field (4:9), and married Ruth (4:13). This union, which birthed a child, *restored Naomi's citizenship* and brought joy to Bethlehem's women, who proclaimed this child as a redeemer for Naomi's family (4:14–15). He was a descendant of David and in the lineage of Jesus.

Similarly, Christ's vow expressed the heavenly DNA of lovingkindness (Phil. 2:6–7). Jesus, in keeping his vow, was born in Bethlehem (2:7) and, in his death (2:8), brought redemption (Heb. 9:12), salvation (9:28), and citizenship in heaven (Eph. 3:20). Through faith, we have come into the lineage or sonship of God, a lineage that includes Jesus, a descendent of David and our ultimate redeemer (Heb. 2:10).

Thank you, our Father, for the redemption we enjoy in Christ, the holy lineage we incredibly share in your Son, and the divine lovingkindness we receive by your grace.

Brian Seim

DECEMBER 15

DOES GOD INTEND TO DWELL AGAIN WITH US?

> And I heard a loud voice from the throne, saying, "Behold, the tabernacle of God is among men, and He will dwell among them, and they shall be His people, and God Himself will be among them.
>
> Revelation 21:3

Reflecting the longing of our hearts, the song *Is He Worthy?* asks this question: "Does God intend to dwell again with us?" When God created the Garden of Eden, he walked in the evening with Adam and Eve, enjoying close fellowship with his people. But after the Fall, humanity was banished from the Garden and their fellowship with God broken. From that moment on, people have been trying to restore what was lost. But *people* are unable to restore it. *We* broke it and *we* can't fix it.

In the tabernacle, God dwelled in the Holy of Holies, his presence represented by a flame. Israel knew that God lived among them. But, even then, they could not enjoy the true fellowship with God, an honour that was reserved for the chief priest once a year when he entered the sacred space on behalf of the people. Then came the Babylonian exile, the ark disappeared, and God fell silent. God's people continued their rituals and sacrifices, but no flame burned, and they wondered together, "Where is our God?"

Into this time of silence a young girl, going about her daily business, was startled by an angel. How bizarre those first moments must have been with her mind racing as she tried to make sense of what she was seeing and hearing. How many times must she have replayed those minutes in her brain in the days that followed! "Did it really happen? What did it mean? Was I dreaming?" But as her body started changing with the new pregnancy, the reality must have begun to sink in: God had given her a child. The words "the holy Child shall be called the Son of God" (Luke 1:35) must have reverberated through her whole being.

With the birth of Christ, God returned to dwell among his people. While on earth, Jesus ate, slept, travelled, laughed, cried, worked, and *truly lived* with his people. When Christ ascended, he sent the Holy Spirit—the church saw the coming of the Holy Spirit and believers received the indwelling of the Holy Spirit—God *with* us and *in* us.

But we have not yet been fully restored to the intimate fellowship of those evening walks in the Garden with God. That is still to come. Jesus' birth was the beginning of the restoration of humanity, not its completion. We long for the day when what is indistinct becomes face to face, what we know in part is known fully. We know that day is coming because God has promised it and, just as he fulfilled his promise to Israel by *sending* Messiah, we can trust him now for the day to come when we will dwell in the House of the Lord forever.

As it has been said, Father, we know it to be true: "Because you have made us for yourself, our hearts are restless until they find their rest in you." Give us such rest, Lord, as we enjoy and await your presence.

Val Lyon

DECEMBER 16

REDEMPTIVE LOVE

> When Jephthah came to his house
> at Mizpah, behold, his daughter was
> coming out to meet him with tambourines
> and with dancing. Now she was his one
> and only child; besides her he had no son
> or daughter.
>
> Judges 11:34

The Christmas season is filled with beauty, music, and cherished traditions. For the Christian, however, the most profound and central theme that resonates through the celebration is love. At the heart of the Christmas story lies the ultimate act of love: God's gift of his only begotten Son for the salvation of humanity (John 3:16). In sending Jesus, God was offering himself, as Christ declares, "I and the Father are one" (10:30). This unfathomable act of divine love is why Christians celebrate as it demonstrates the depth of God's commitment to redeeming mankind.

The sacrificial nature of God's love is highlighted in Isaiah 53:10: "But the LORD was pleased to crush" his Son. God willingly endured the pain of his Son's suffering for our redemption. The selfless offering of Christ was a divine necessity to reconcile sinful humanity with a holy God.

A contrasting narrative can be found in the story of Jephthah in Judges 11. Jephthah, a judge of Israel, vowed that, if he were victorious in battle, he would offer as a burnt sacrifice the first thing that greeted him upon his return home. Tragically, it was his only daughter who met him and what should have been a moment of celebration became a time of unimaginable sorrow.

The differences between these two stories could not be starker. Jephthah's vow led to regret, grief, and death but God willingly gave himself to bring life, joy, and salvation. Jephthah's act was one of rashness and personal tragedy while God's was one of grace and selflessness. Jephthah's daughter paid the ultimate price for her father's promise, while Christ died for our transgressions.

This Christmas season, let us choose to celebrate Yahweh, the covenant-making God, who gave himself in the person of Christ to redeem us from death and bring us into eternal life. As 2 Corinthians 5:21 beautifully states, "He made Him who knew no sin to be sin on our behalf, so that we might become the righteousness of God in Him." Through Christ, when God looks upon us, he no longer sees our sin but sees his Son—holy, righteous, and redeemed.

Lord Jesus, you are more worthy of celebration and honour than we can give but we offer now what we can. We worship this day for what you gave—your life—and for what you give—eternal life.

Simon Githae

DECEMBER 17

THE PROMISE OF GLORY

> God, after He spoke long ago to the fathers in the prophets in many portions and in many ways, in these last days has spoken to us in His Son.
>
> Hebrews 1:1–2

Jesus is the radiance of the glory of God. Some may ask, "How is that so?" Well, he is the satisfaction of anticipation in the Old Testament and the continuation of God's self-revelation in the New Testament. "In these last days" God has spoken through his Son and the Son has the final word.

In ancient times it was tradition to give the first-born son a significant inheritance. Consistently and climactically, God appointed Jesus "the firstborn of all creation" (Col. 1:15) and "heir of all things" (Heb. 1:2). John 1:3 adds that, "All things came into being through Him, and apart from Him nothing came into being that has come into being." So, Jesus Christ is the creator and owner of everything!

It is wondrous to think how Mary must have felt holding her Lord in her arms at his birth, treasuring and pondering all these things in her heart (Luke 2:19). Or how Joseph must have felt seeing the many shepherds show up at the birthplace of Jesus (2:8–21), verifying that he was the Saviour as the angel had spoken to him (1:18–25).

When driving in the northern parts of Canada, Inukshuk figures are a familiar sight. The Inuit and other First Nations people have been creating these impressive stone markers for generations. Although they can represent many meanings, the word *Inukshuk* means "in the likeness of a human"—*inuk* meaning "person" and *suk,* "substitute."

As Christians, we believe that Jesus came not just in the likeness of a human, but as a person, fully God and fully human, to be our substitute. Jesus is the radiance of the glory of God because he came as our substitute and "suffered once for our sins, the righteous for the unrighteous" (1 Pet. 3:18), offering eternal life to all who believe in him for it. Jesus is the exact representation of God and his perfect plan of redemption: the promise of salvation. Nothing can be more glorious than this!

God holds the universe together by the power of his word. Jesus *is* the Word (John 1:1) and *we* are part of the universe he sustains (Heb. 1:3). Not only can he hold all things in his hands but, for those who believe, he savingly holds them in his hands too. Jesus is the "Light of the world" (John 8:12). He is radiant because he is the only Saviour born to us, the one who offered "purification for sins" to reconcile sinners to our holy God. This is why he was born and willingly went to the cross for us.

God in heaven, we praise you for your power—power to create and to sustain, power to save and to keep. May our awe of your greatness be refreshed this season.

Penelope Jane Jolin

DECEMBER 18

THE SIMPLICITY OF THE GIFT

*For the wages of sin is death,
but the free gift of God is eternal
life in Christ Jesus our Lord.*

Romans 6:23

One year for Christmas, a roommate and I decided to bless two tenants in our home who could not see their families over the holidays. It started as a spontaneous set of stockings filled with chocolate and grew to include other small tokens that spoke to their unique personalities. We grew in excitement as Christmas Day approached when we would be able to reveal our little surprise. Before we left town for our family celebrations, we placed the treasure-laden stockings in the kitchen to be discovered by our nomadic roommates.

When we returned home post-holiday, can you guess what we found on the kitchen table? Two more stockings! We were disappointed to learn that our spontaneous gift had not sparked excitement on Christmas morning but, instead, guilt! Our roommates, upon seeing our thoughtfulness and generosity, had rushed out to "guilt-gift" in reciprocation because they felt so terrible about not having gifts for us. We did not want to introduce the pressure of a gift exchange, but our spontaneity certainly backfired!

It has become a cultural custom to, at this time of year, participate in gift *exchange*. Because of that, it can be a challenge to experience the unique blessing of a gift *received*. But it is this season when we remember the free gift of God—eternal life in Christ Jesus our Lord—and we get to practice the art of receiving.

Lord God, you are my strength and my song! Thank you for the gift of everlasting life, a gift that cost you dearly to offer and costs us nothing to receive. What grace! What mercy!

Sarah George

DECEMBER 19

JUSTICE AND MERCY

> "Therefore the LORD Himself will give you a sign: Behold, a virgin will be with child and bear a son, and she will call His name Immanuel."
>
> Isaiah 7:14

Whenever I reflect on the miraculous conception of Jesus, I can't help but think of Joseph and what he must have gone through. No matter how often I try to convince myself that I would have acted like him, my inner voice tells me, "Stop deceiving yourself!"

Joseph was betrothed to Mary, likely filled with dreams of their future together, plans of settling down and raising a family. Then, out of nowhere, he finds out Mary is pregnant. In that moment, his world must have shattered. He would naturally think, "How could you, Mary? How could you betray our love?" And had Mary explained that the Holy Spirit was responsible for the conception it may have sounded absurd to him. Like any rational man, Joseph assumed infidelity and considered ending their engagement.

Matthew 1:19 captures the pivotal moment: "And Joseph her husband, being a righteous man and not wanting to disgrace her, planned to send her away secretly." Joseph, as a just man, felt he needed to do the right thing—end the relationship. But it's the second part of the verse that truly challenges me. He was also compassionate. Despite believing that Mary had been unfaithful, he didn't seek to shame her. Instead, he chose to quietly end things to protect her dignity.

This is where Joseph's character deeply resonates. Most of us would want to proclaim our innocence, to let everyone know we weren't the guilty party. But Joseph waived that right. He was ready to follow the law while still showing compassion, even in the face of hurt and betrayal.

In Joseph, we see a powerful example of balancing justice with mercy. No wonder God sent an angel to reassure him that he was in control. Joseph's story reminds us that even when we feel wronged, we can choose to respond with compassion, regardless of who is at fault.

When we are wronged, Father, help us to remember that your Son was wronged also and that bearing up under such injustice in your strength is an opportunity to share in our Saviour's sufferings.

Godsgrace Agu

DECEMBER 20

WALKING WITH AND WAITING FOR GOD

> At that very moment she came up and
> began giving thanks to God,
> and continued to speak of Him
> to all those who were looking for the
> redemption of Jerusalem.
>
> Luke 2:38

As a prophet, Anna was spiritually blessed to speak to people about God regularly. She was also a widow of great age (Luke 2:36). Widowhood in Jesus' time was extremely difficult. To make a difficult situation more difficult, no mention of offspring leads us to believe that Anna was also childless. Therefore, she likely lived most of her life in poverty and vulnerability, eighty-four years or more! But Anna had a very intimate relationship with God, worshipping him daily. She dedicated almost her entire life to serving God on the temple grounds. "She never left the temple, serving night and day with fastings and prayers" (2:37).

Readers of Luke's Gospel are invited to picture Anna walking around the temple routinely because of the nature of her ministry. But the day recorded for us in Luke 2 is no ordinary day. It is no coincidence that she was there "at the very moment" (2:38) to witness the encounter between Simeon and baby Jesus (2:25–35). The timing is impeccable! God's providential timing!

When Anna saw Jesus, her first reaction was to "give thanks to God" (2:38). For a long time, she had eagerly waited for the Messiah. Certainly, she was grateful and joyful to witness her prayer becoming a reality! This wonderful experience propelled her to tell everyone about the arrival of the Lord: she "spoke about the child to all who were looking forward to the redemption of Jerusalem" (2:38). God had orchestrated the whole event, and it had blessed Anna beyond any imagination.

As the psalmist declares, "How blessed is the one whom you choose and bring near to you to dwell in your courts. We will be satisfied with the goodness of your house, your holy temple" (Ps. 65:4). We can expect great blessings when we practice walking with God every day. God uses ordinary people to accomplish his extraordinary plan.

"One thing I ask from the LORD, this only do I seek: that I may dwell in the house of the LORD all the days of my life, to gaze on the beauty of the LORD and to seek him in his temple" (Ps. 27:4).

Lord Jesus, help us to be a blessed people who daily abide in you, walk closely by you, grow in our longing to be with you, and eagerly and patiently wait for you.

Alice Popovich

DECEMBER 21

FROM LIGHT TO LIFE

> When Jesus spoke again to the people, he said, "I am the light of the world. Whoever follows me will never walk in darkness, but will have the light of life."
>
> John 8:12 NIV

"Joseph's Dream" is an oil painting from 1645 that most art historians attribute to the great Dutch master, Rembrandt. For me, it's one of Rembrandt's most powerful and moving images related to the birth of Christ. The painting depicts the second dream of Joseph where the angel warns Joseph to leave Bethlehem and flee to Egypt because King Herod is searching for the child to kill him (Matt. 2:13).

The painting shows Joseph and Mary looking completely exhausted. Rembrandt uses somber earthy tones throughout the painting that remind us of the dark and impoverished world Jesus was born into. The darkness and filth are so dense that, at first glance, it looks like the darkness may overcome the light.

At second glance, however, we see this is not the case. The dark earth tones give way to radiant golden hues that illuminate the face of a tired Mary and the angel who places a gentle and reassuring hand on Joseph's shoulder to urge him to head to Egypt.

The painting invites us into an intimate moment where the divine meets humanity. Today, this same God will do for you and me what he did for Joseph and Mary. When we are exhausted and weary of this world, Christ will meet us in our need, promises to be with us through the ups and downs of life, and gives us his strength and guidance for the road ahead.

This Christmas may we have a renewed sense of wonder that the Son of God willingly came into this world to be the antidote to sin and darkness. And may Christ shine through us so others may be called out of darkness into his wonderful light.

Spirit of God, fill us afresh with an overwhelming and motivating awe of our Saviour, that we may be salt and light in a world that desperately needs both. All this for the glory of Christ and the fame of his name.

Elaine Irwin

DECEMBER 22

FAITH IN GOD'S PROVISION

> "Take now your son, your only son, whom you love, Isaac, and go to the land of Moriah, and offer him there as a burnt offering on one of the mountains of which I will tell you."
>
> Genesis 22:2

The story of Abraham's journey to fatherhood is one with which most Christians are familiar. By faith, he and his wife, Sarah, waited years for the child God promised them (Heb. 11:8–11). In Genesis 21, we read that the now-elderly couple finally welcomed that son but that their joy was to be short-lived as, in the next chapter, God asks Abraham to give Isaac back in sacrifice. Amazingly, this new father again wholeheartedly trusted the Lord for provision, even when it seemed impossible and unintelligible. Just as the patriarch was about to slaughter Isaac, an angel stopped his hand and showed him a ram he could use instead (Gen. 22:10–13). Isaac's life was spared.

This event could have had a tragic ending but, instead, Abraham and his family experienced God's timely provision, love, and faithfulness. To commemorate the event, Abraham named the place of his son's near-death experience "the LORD will provide" (22:14).

God told Abraham to sacrifice "your son, your only son, whom you love" (22:2). This heavy request foreshadowed what God would do years later: sacrifice *his* only Son, the one *he* loves, for the sake of the world (John 3:16). Jesus Christ, the ultimate Son of promise, came not to condemn the world but to bring salvation (3:17). The gift of Christ speaks to God's timely provision and faithfulness. The Father loved us so much that he sent his Son to be sacrificed in our place (1 Pet. 3:18). The same way he had provided Abraham with a ram, the Father sent the Lamb of God to take away our sins (John 1:29).

Christmas is a wonderful time of year marked by great joy, love, generosity, and family time. But the season can also be a stark reminder of our personal needs, especially if any of these essential things are lacking in one's life. Perhaps you do not have a loving family with whom you can share the joy. Maybe you are lacking gifts under the tree or a meal for your loved ones. Such deficiencies can certainly steal joy and dampen the festive mood.

This Christmas, instead of focusing on what we lack, let us look back to Genesis 22 and be reminded of God's timely provision of his Son, Jesus Christ, the only reason for the season. Like the father of faith, Abraham, let us have unwavering faith that God will provide and meet all our needs as we celebrate the gift of Christ this joyous season.

Lord of Hosts, you have lovingly given your children all we need in your Son and by your Spirit. Grant us, we pray, a heart of contentment and gratitude, of faith in your present provision and hope in your future provision.

Bertha Githae

DECEMBER 23

THE WORD BECAME MAN TO SAVE US

> And the Word became flesh, and dwelt among us, and we saw His glory, glory as of the only begotten from the Father, full of grace and truth.
>
> John 1:14

John, one of Jesus' disciples, writes about the mysterious person called "the Word." He describes who the Word *is* and what the Word *does*. He was with God in the beginning and is God himself. All things were created through the Word and the Word has become flesh.

John goes on to say that this Word will bring light to humanity living in darkness and revelation to a people separated from God. At the time of his arrival, Israel was living under Roman occupation and had been led astray by corrupt shepherds. Yet, the *real* problem they were facing was—and always has been—sin, the power of darkness that separates people from God Almighty. Human beings, without exception, have all sinned.

However, as hopeless as this seems, hope shone forth in the bright Word. The Word became flesh so that he may dwell among sinning people. By taking on a human nature he has come to end darkness by offering himself as the means for satisfying the penalty for sin and fixing the problem of sin. It is not a surprise that John writes, "and we saw His glory,

glory as of the only begotten from the Father, full of grace and truth."

What a testimony to bear and share with God's people! John, along with the other disciples and eyewitnesses, was able to see the living God through the person of the Son whom we know as Jesus Christ. This person of God has brought to his people grace and truth. He offers a grace that brings salvation to all who believe in him and truth that brings justice to satisfy God's judgement for sin.

We can all take comfort in the Word made flesh because he has come to save us from our sins and to cleanse us from all unrighteousness. One day he would be sacrificed and killed for bearing our sins so that God's judgement for sin is fully satisfied and all who have trusted in Jesus will have eternal life and no longer dwell in darkness but in the light of our Saviour.

Our God and Saviour, as David once prayed so we pray now: you are our lamp and you, O Lord, turn our darkness into light. We thank you and praise you for rescuing sinners like us, saving sinners like us, enlivening sinners like us!

Brett Harris

DECEMBER 24

WORTHY OF OUR PRAISE

> And suddenly there appeared with the
> angel a multitude of the heavenly host
> praising God and saying, "Glory to God in
> the highest, and on earth peace among
> men with whom He is pleased."
>
> Luke 2:13–14

On a quiet, beautiful, starry night, the world was unaware of the momentous event unfolding—the birth of our Saviour. While we often picture a stable and a baby in a manger, let us shift our focus to the skies for a few moments. After Jesus was born, the very first thing recorded is an angelic announcement and a chorus of praise from a heavenly host.

Luke 2:13–14 says, "And suddenly there appeared with the angel a multitude of the heavenly host praising God and saying, 'Glory to God in the highest, and on earth peace among men with whom He is pleased!'" At the arrival of our Saviour, heaven couldn't remain silent, immediately erupting in praise. If the angels reacted this way to Jesus' coming, how much more should we, those created to worship, continuously have his praises on our lips? As God has said through Isaiah, "The people whom I formed for Myself will declare My praise" (43:21).

Just as his earthly life began with angelic praise, his earthly ministry ended with people shouting his praises. When the Pharisees tried to silence his supporters, Jesus declared that if people didn't praise him, nature would: "I tell you, if these become silent, the stones will cry out" (see Luke 19:37–40). What a powerful image! If we aren't moved to worship, creation itself will rise up to fill the void!

That "little baby" we picture in the manger is truly our Lord and Saviour, our God who is worthy of all praise. Psalm 105:2 reminds us to "Sing to Him, sing praises to Him; speak of all His wonders."

Let us not leave the honour of praising him to the rocks. Instead, take time to worship, sing, and proclaim his wondrous deeds to the world. He is, always has been, and always will be worthy of our praise!

Praise the Lord in his sanctuary and in his mighty expanse. Praise him for his mighty deeds and his excellent greatness. Indeed, let all that has breath praise the Lord!

Phil, Stephanie, Michael,
Christina, Joy, and Joanna Wahab

DECEMBER 25

WHEN CAME THE FULLNESS OF TIME

> But when the fullness of time came, God
> sent forth His Son, born of a woman, born
> under the Law, so that He might redeem
> those who were under the Law, that we
> might receive the adoption as sons.
>
> Galatians 4:4–5

God is glorious. The pages of the Old Testament are filled with people falling on their faces before him and of people crying out for their lives because they've seen him. Moses removed his sandals when on holy ground and his face shone after speaking with God. This God is greater than our understanding, higher than our ways, more powerful than we can imagine. We cannot abide in his presence—he is too holy—and yet his plan involved bringing his physical presence to us.

According to his plan, time reached its fullness when the Creator became part of his creation. This holy, mighty God decided to engage with his rebellious creatures in the most personal way: God sent his son to be born of a woman. The infinite confined himself in the human experience. Fully God and fully man in the person of Jesus.

The author of justice and ultimate authority was "born under the law." We had sinned, forever separating ourselves from our perfect God, forever convicted under a charge we could never repay. This is what the Law made clear: we stand forever condemned. In becoming man, Jesus submitted himself to his law to fulfil the requirement we could not meet, so that he could clear the charge in full. As the Christmas carol joyously proclaims: "God and sinners, reconciled."

Paying this debt is just the beginning. As well as freeing us from the Law, Jesus came to adopt us as his own. Rather than being struck down in the presence of God, we are welcomed into his arms and given a heavenly inheritance. Rather than being banished as strangers from the Almighty God, we have unrestricted access to him. He is our Father, and we are his children.

Advent is a time of anticipation. Every day we look forward, counting down until Christmas morning. In Galatians, Paul reminds us that from the moment of Adam's sin, creation began counting down to the moment God would walk the earth so that he could redeem it.

Centuries later, Advent also reminds us to look forward to when time will reach a new fullness, and our Saviour will return to this earth and finish the work he began.

> *Mild he lays his glory by,*
> *Born that man no more may die*
> *Born to raise the sons of earth,*
> *Born to give them second birth.*
> *Hark the herald angels sing,*
> *Glory to the newborn King.*

Father, as we celebrate the humble advent of your Son, help us to also anticipate the climactic advent of your Son. As we look back with gratitude, may we also look ahead with joy.

Rebecca Roebuck

GLORY TO GOD IN THE HIGHEST

Father, Son, and Holy Spirit; God eternal and saver of souls, we praise you this season for your generosity, love, and grace. Help us, we pray, live lives that honour and reflect you to a world that needs light.

John Jones